Rock Harmonica

Taught by Al Ek

Text by Steve Gorenberg
DVD presentation by Al Ek

ISBN 978-160378-897-7

Visit our website at
www.cherrylaneprint.com

Contents

Introduction

Welcome to world of rock harmonica. In this book and DVD program we'll explore essential harmonica techniques and theory, and show you how to play in the style of some of your favorite artists. This book is broken down into two sections. In the first part, we'll explore all of the harmonica basics you need to get started, as well as some advanced techniques like bends, vibrato, and trills. You'll also learn some simple scale theory and how to play in different positions and keys on the harmonica. In the second section, we'll present a series of songs and solos in the styles of some of the classic rock harmonica greats.

We've presented all of the music and examples in this book using a system of numbers and symbols specifically designed for harmonica notation. This program doesn't require you to have any previous background in music; there's no traditional music notation used. Each section of the book coincides with an easy-to-follow lesson on the accompanying DVD, giving you detailed instructions on how to master all of the techniques you'll need. There's a handy chart in the back of the book showing all of the notes on the harmonica for each key. To get you started, we recommend getting the four most popular harmonicas: G, A, C and F. Most of the examples in this book can be played using those four keys. As you advance through the program, you can add other keys to your collection.

About the Author

Musician, performer, bandleader, teacher, and guitarist Al Ek has been a mainstay on the Las Vegas music scene for years. His career started over 30 years ago when he was playing harmonica in Milwaukee and Chicago blues clubs. He later played in the Shuffle-Aires and opened for such legendary blues and roots acts as Johnny Winter, Fabulous Thunderbirds, Los Lobos, Lonnie Brooks, and NRBQ, among others. In 1992 he accepted an offer to play in the "American Superstar" show at the famous Las Vegas Flamingo. He has since recorded numerous sessions for various Las Vegas artists as well as radio and television spots. Ek currently teaches at A.J.'s Music, is guitarist for the House of Blues Schoolhouse Band, and plays and tours with the Pete Contino Band.

Harmonica Basics

Low to High

Let's get started with some rudimentary music theory. If you've never played a musical instrument before, this will help you to understand the musical terminology we'll be using throughout the program.

There are seven different letter-name notes in the musical alphabet: A-B-C-D-E-F-G. These notes are called *natural notes*. The distance in pitch between two notes is called an *interval*. For now, the two types of intervals we'll be concerned with are *half steps* and *whole steps*. Half steps occur in the musical alphabet between the notes B and C, and between the notes E and F. All of the other intervals are whole steps.

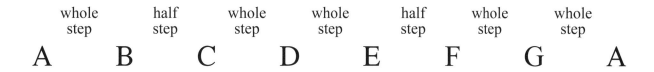

After counting up from A to G, we get to a higher sounding A and can continue to count up higher through the alphabet again from there. The distance from that first A to the next A is called an *octave*.

To *sharp* a note is to go up in pitch; to *flat* a note is to go down in pitch. Sharp and flat notes occur between most of the natural notes in the musical alphabet. A sharp (♯) raises a note by a half step; a flat (♭) lowers a note by a half step. For example, the note in between A and B can be called either an A♯ or a B♭; it's actually the same sounding note with two different names. The use of sharps or flats are usually determined by the scale or key. The complete musical alphabet (including all of the sharps and flats) consists of 12 different notes. If you play all 12 notes in order, you are playing what's known as a *chromatic scale*.

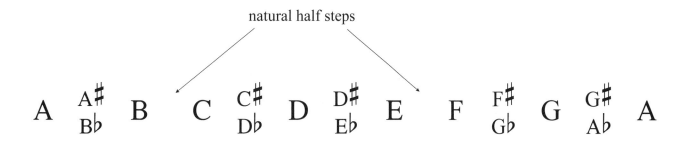

Chromatic Scales

Harmonicas are often referred to as *harps*, or *mouth harps*. The lowest key harmonica is G. From G on up, there is a different harmonica for each step of the chromatic scale. The most popular harmonicas, and the ones that you'll need to get started with, are G, A, C, and F. Most of the songs in this book (with the exception of two) can be played on those four harmonicas. The D harmonica is also useful, followed by the E♭, D♭ and B♭ harmonicas, which are used in two songs later in this book.

The lower sounding harmonicas are G, A♭, A, and B♭. These lower-key harmonicas are generally softer and require more air to bend notes. Since these are lower-pitched harmonicas, their entire range can be utilized without sounding too abrasive.

The middle-range harmonicas are B, C, D♭, and D. These are the most all-around versatile harps and the easiest to play. They're moderately loud, easier to bend notes on, and the higher register is still useful without sounding too shrill.

The higher sounding harmonicas are E♭, E, F, and F♯. The harps in this register are quite a bit louder than the others, and the higher register tends to have a shrill, piercing tone.

Tongue Blocking

Let's start by learning how to play individual notes on the harmonica. For each hole on the harmonica there are two notes readily available—one blown and one drawn. First let's isolate hole 2 by using one finger from each hand to block holes 1 and 3. Inhale (draw) on hole 2 to play the note and get a feel for how much air is required to achieve a clear, steady tone. To play an individual note without using your fingers, you're going to utilize a technique called *tongue blocking* to block unwanted notes with your tongue and the edges of your mouth. Place the tip of your tongue in hole 1 to completely block that hole. Hole 2 should remain open, just to the right of your tongue, and the right edge of your mouth should block off hole 3. Once you've got the draw note for hole 2 sounding good, try to exhale (blow) and produce the blow note for hole 2.

Instead of using standard musical notation in this book, we'll employ a system of numbers and symbols specifically designed for harmonica notation. The numbers below designate which holes on the harmonica to play. The down arrow represents a draw note (inhale and draw the air down into your lungs). The up arrow represents a blow note (exhale and blow the air up and out of your lungs).

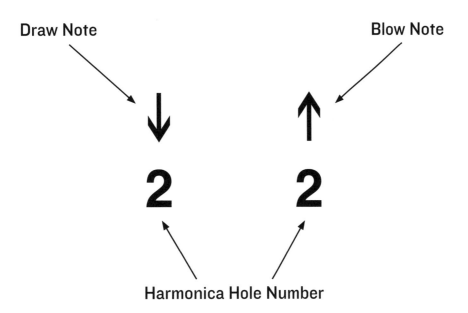

C Major Scale

Now let's use the C harmonica to play a C major scale. This is known as playing in *1st position*—playing in the harmonica's original key. Practice playing the ascending and descending C major scales below until you're used to switching from hole to hole, and the individual notes sounds clean and clear.

Ascending C Major Scale

Descending C Major Scale

The major scale contains seven different letter-name notes. We'll refer to these different notes by number according to their step of the scale in relation to the 1st step (also known as the *tonic*). For example, if we're talking about the 3rd in the key of C, then we're referring to the note E. If we're talking about the 5th and the 7th, we're referring to the notes G and B. These scale degrees are not to be confused with the numbered holes of the harmonica.

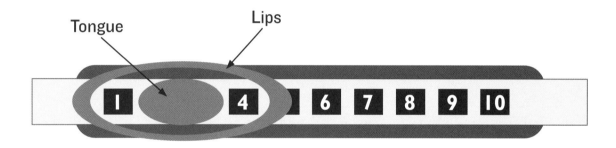

Root	2nd	3rd	4th	5th	6th	7th	Octave
C	D	E	F	G	A	B	C

Playing Octaves

Here's an advanced technique you can use to play two notes simultaneously that are an octave apart. Using the C harmonica, we're going to play the blow notes C at hole 1 and the C an octave higher at hole 4. Your mouth should be stretched wider across holes 1 through 4, while using your tongue to block holes 2 and 3.

Throughout this book, we'll use stacked numbers to show when two holes on the harmonica are played simultaneously. The notation below indicates holes 1 and 4 should be blown simultaneously.

The draw notes at holes 1 and 4 are also octaves. You can also play blow-note octaves across the rest of the harmonica by using the same technique. There are octaves at holes 2 and 5, holes 3 and 6, holes 4 and 7, and continuously on up through the full range of the harmonica.

Draw-Note Bends

Bending a note on the harmonica causes the pitch to go down. Most harmonica bends are achieved on draw notes. There are seven additional notes that aren't on the harmonica that can be generated through draw-note bends. To bend a note, increase the air flow while slightly curving your tongue at the edges into a u-shape or taco shape. The curved arrow below indicates a whole step draw-note bend. Draw-holes 2 and 3 can be bent down a whole step.

On all harmonicas, draw-holes 1, 4 and 6 can be bent down a half step. The underscored diagonal arrow below indicates a half step draw-note bend.

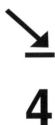

Half step draw-note bends can also be achieved on holes 2 and 3 by controlling the technique and airflow. Use your ear to identify the correct pitches, and practice refining the bend technique to execute the different half and whole step bends.

Blow-Note Bends

Blow-note bends can be generated on holes 8, 9, and 10 of the harmonica. Hole 8 can be bent down a half step, while holes 9 and 10 can be bent down a half step or a whole step. The symbols below indicate, respectively, half and whole step blow-note bends.

Vibrato Notes

Vibrato can be applied to blow notes, draw notes, and bend notes. Harmonica vibrato is achieved much in the same way that singers add vibrato to vocal notes. Apply a slight quiver or shimmy to the column of air as you draw or blow a sustained note. The symbols below represent, respectively, draw-note vibrato and blow-note vibrato.

Vibrato can also be applied to bend notes. One common technique is to apply vibrato to a half step bend at draw-hole 3. The symbol below represents vibrato on a half step draw-note bend.

Worble or Trill Notes

Worbles (also referred to as *trills*) can be performed by evenly oscillating between two adjacent notes on the harmonica. Perform this technique by very slightly moving your head back and forth, and moving the harmonica back and forth in a counter motion. The symbols below represent, respectively, draw-note worbles and blow-note worbles. In this book the symbols will be centered above the two harmonica hole numbers.

Playing in 2nd Position

Playing the same key harmonica as the key of the song is known as playing in 1st position. In 1st position all of the prominent scale tones are blow notes on the harmonica. If instead we use a harmonica that's a perfect 4th (or two and a half steps) above the original key, we can play in that song's key by playing in 2nd position. In 2nd position, the prominent scale tones—the tonic, 3rd, and 5th steps of the scale—are played using draw notes, giving us more opportunities for expression and articulation using bends and vibrato.

The following example is a slight variation of the C major scale, played in 2nd position on the F harmonica. The seventh step of the scale in 2nd position is a flatted 7th, which gives the scale more of a blues flavor.

The table below shows which harmonica should be used to play in 2nd position for each of the 12 keys.

Key of Song	C	D♭	D	E♭	E	F	F♯	G	A♭	A	B♭	B
2nd Position Harmonica	F	F♯	G	A♭	A	B♭	B	C	D♭	D	E♭	E

Playing in 3rd Position

Playing in 3rd position gives us an altered minor scale, useful for playing songs in minor keys. The harmonica used to play in 3rd position is one whole step lower than the key of the song. The 3rd position version of the minor scale contains a raised 6th. The scale below is an altered A minor scale, played on a G harmonica.

The table below shows which harmonica should be used to play in 3rd position for each of the 12 keys.

Key of Song	Cm	D♭m	Dm	E♭m	Em	Fm	F♯m	Gm	A♭m	Am	B♭m	Bm
3rd Position Harmonica	B♭	B	C	D♭	D	E♭	E	F	F♯	G	A♭	A

Songs

Neil Young

Our first song is a simple melody in the style of Neil Young. We're going to start off with the G harmonica in 1st position playing in the key of G. Follow along with the DVD to get a feel for the rhythm and phrasing. The melody can be broken down into four sections, shown in the notation below—reading left to right, the first line of music contains sections 1 & 2; the second line contains sections 3 & 4. Practice slowly until you have each part memorized and your tone is consistent throughout.

1st Position – G Harmonica

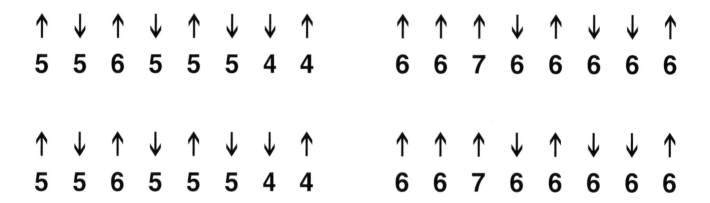

Let's take the same melody and move it to 2nd position using a C harp. A few of the notes are now played using bends, making the song a little more difficult. The advantage is that we've moved some of the key notes to draw holes, making it easier to manipulate the tone. We've added draw-note vibrato to the last note of each line.

2nd Position – C Harmonica

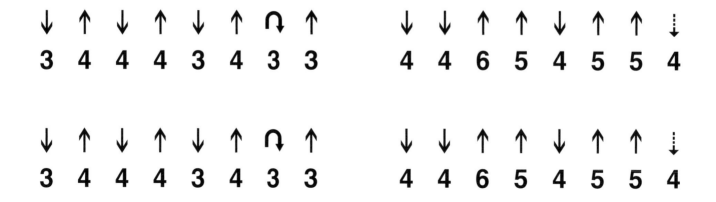

Once you're accustomed to playing the melody in 2nd position, try the following solo. It's a slightly more complicated variation of the melody with quicker phrasing. Pay close attention to the bends at the beginning of the first two phrases, making sure to bend consistently to the correct pitches. The first two lines of the solo are similar, and are then transposed an octave higher for the last two lines.

2nd Position – C Harmonica

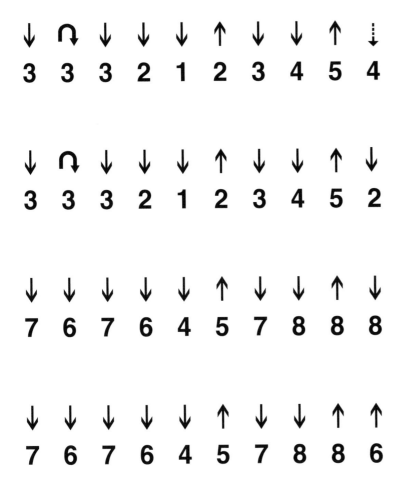

Bob Dylan

Here's a selection in the key of C in the style of Bob Dylan. We'll start off with a basic melody in 1st position using a C harp. This song incorporates a few half step bends at the end of the 2nd and 4th lines at draw-hole 4. The technique used here is to first sustain the regular draw note, then gradually bend the note.

1st Position – C Harmonica

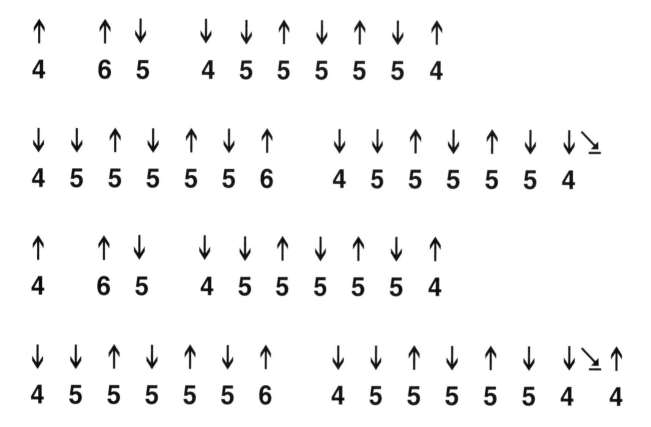

Once you've learned the above melody, let's take it into 2nd position on an F harp. This requires a few more whole step bends to achieve some of the key notes.

2nd Position – F Harmonica

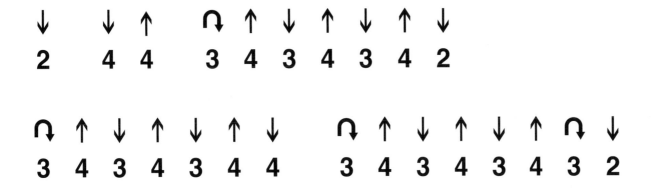

You'll notice that the 2nd position version of the melody doesn't sound quite as good as the 1st position version, mostly due to the placement of the bends on sustained notes. The benefits of 2nd position are the options available for playing variations and solos. The example below demonstrates how the draw notes and bends in 2nd position can be used to your advantage in a solo.

2nd Position – F Harmonica

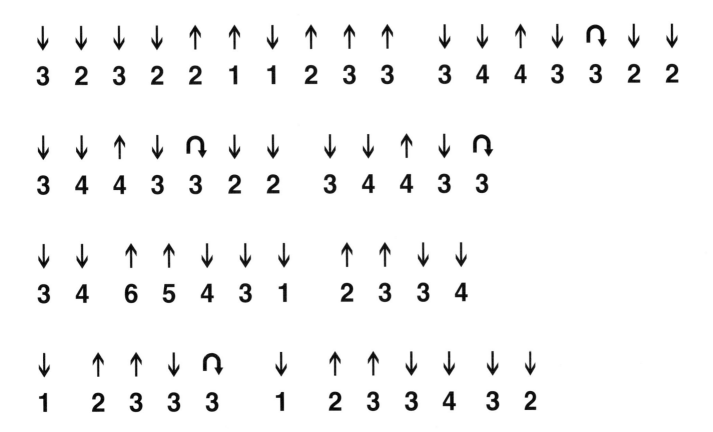

Once you've got all of the parts down, try putting it all together by playing the melody and solo consecutively. If you prefer to play the original melody in 1st position, you can easily perform this live by using two harmonicas. Play the first section with a C harp in 1st position, then switch to an F harp for the solo.

The Beatles

This next example in C is reminiscent of early Beatles songs. John Lennon usually played in 1st position, so let's first learn the melody on the C harp. The slight bends near the end of the 2nd and 3rd lines are used to slide into the regular draw notes, giving the phrases a more vocal flavor.

1st Position – C Harmonica

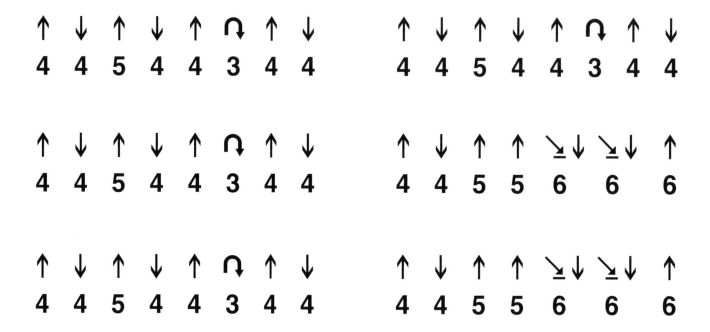

Now let's move the melody into 2nd position using the F harmonica. You can see right away how much more difficult this is to play in 2nd position because of the many required bend notes. The benefit is that some of the important scale tones have now been moved to draw notes, allowing you to play the melody with a more expressive, saxophone-like quality.

2nd Position – F Harmonica

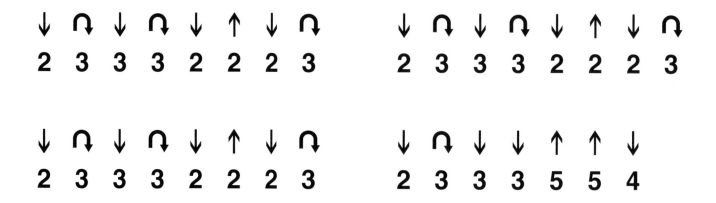

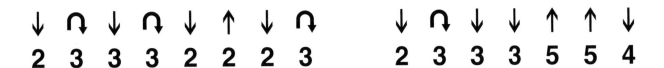

The solo below incorporates a few new techniques. The stacked numbers on the first line represent chords, and are played with slight pre-bends to slide into the notes. This is the classic harmonica train impersonation sound. At the end of the 2nd and 3rd lines, the long diagonal arrows represent steady glissandos or *slides*. While playing draw note 5, slide your mouth down the length of the harmonica to the next indicated hole. We refer to these as *piano slides* because they have a similar effect as running your fingers down the keys of a piano. Piano slides will be used extensively throughout the rest of the book.

2nd Position – F Harmonica

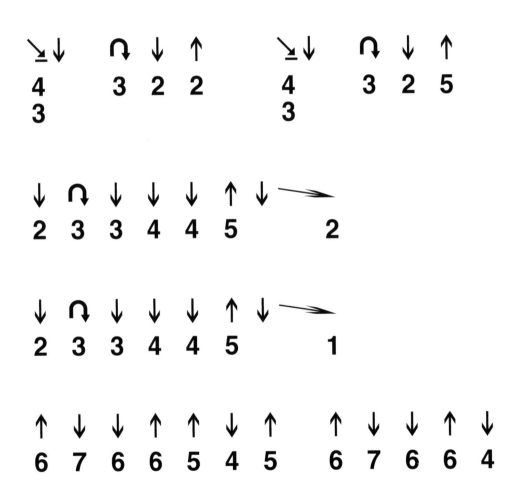

Billy Joel

This key of C example in 3/4 time is in the style of Billy Joel. Like the previous examples, we'll start out by learning the melody in 1st position on a C harp.

1st Position – C Harmonica

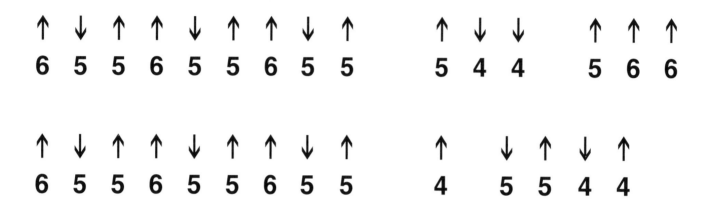

Now let's move the melody into 2nd position on an F harp and incorporate some bends and vibrato.

2nd Position – F Harmonica

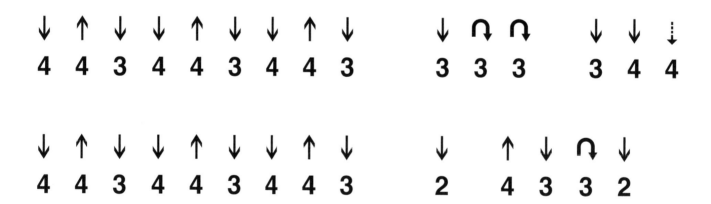

Here's a neat little solo that clearly demonstrates the advantages of being in 2nd position. The smaller size bend arrows indicate slight grace note bends, used here to add some character to the solo and give it that saxophone-style sound. A *grace note* is an extra note added as an embellishment.

2nd Position – F Harmonica

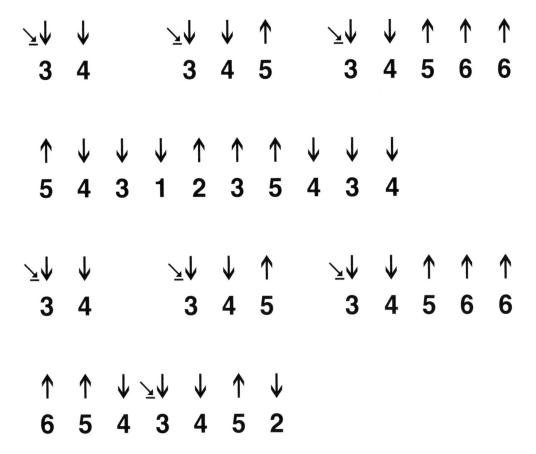

Supertramp

Until now we've played songs in 1st position and then showed you how to transpose them to 2nd position to make them more versatile. Now we'll advance into more complicated songs that originate in 2nd position and use advanced techniques in the basic melody. The following example in the style of Supertramp is in the key of C, so we'll use an F harp in 2nd position. The first two lines of the example incorporate some familiar half step bends and a piano slide. The last two lines should be played with a more *staccato* feel, cutting the notes short and impersonating a chicken cluck sound.

2nd Position – F Harmonica

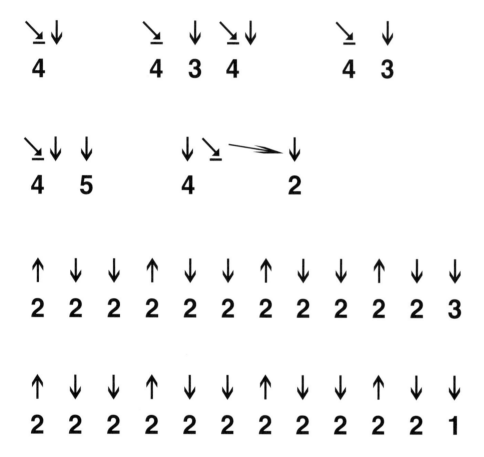

Here's another variation of the melody in 2nd position to try out. This one uses piano slides in an upward direction from hole 1 to hole 4. The first slide goes up to hole 4, then does an immediate half step bend with a gradual release back to the natural pitch at hole 4, all on the same sustained note.

2nd Position – F Harmonica

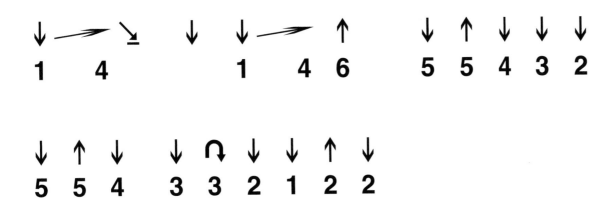

Finally, here's a third variation incorporating some draw-note trills and blow-note worbles in the second line. Once you've got all of the variations down, try stringing them all together into one long solo.

2nd Position – F Harmonica

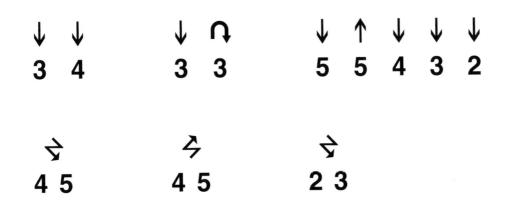

The Romantics

Here's an example of a melody in the style of the pop-rock group the Romantics. We're going to be playing in the key of E using an A harp in 2nd position. The first part below is fairly straightforward, starting out with some more worbles at holes 4 and 5.

2nd Position – A Harmonica

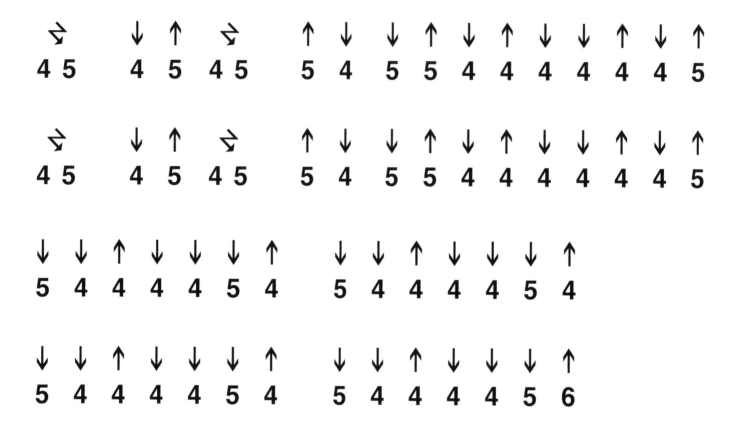

Now let's try a solo using some of the familiar techniques from the previous songs. Since the A harp is one of the lower harmonica keys, you may need to adjust your technique and airflow to produce clear and accurate bends. This solo is in a question/answer format—the first line of the example sets it up and the second line replies.

2nd Position – A Harmonica

↓ ↘ ↓ ↓ ↘ ↓ ↑ ↓ ↓ ↘ ——→ ↓
4 3 4 3 4 3 6 5 4   2

↓ ↘ ↓ ↓ ↘ ↓ ↑ ↓ ↑ ↓
4 3 4 3 4 3 6 5 4 4

Here's a second Romantics solo that utilizes some worbles and piano slides. Once you've got this one down, put it together with the previous example to create one continuous solo.

2nd Position – A Harmonica

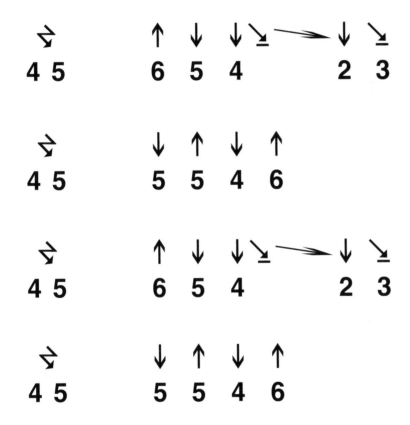

Tom Petty

Now let's try something in 3rd position. This is a song in the style of Tom Petty in the key of A minor, so we'll be using a G harp. The first few lines start off with piano slides going up into the draw notes. There's also some good examples of draw-note vibrato. The last line contains the familiar grace note bend technique at draw hole 6.

3rd Position – G Harmonica

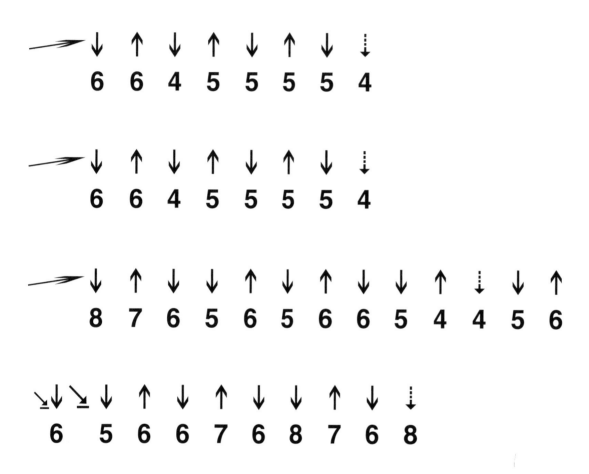

Led Zeppelin

Our next selection is in the style of Led Zeppelin, played in the key of E using an A harmonica in 2nd position. This example is played over a standard 12-bar blues shuffle. A *shuffle* is a rhythm based on a triplet subdivision of the beat rather than a division of the beat into halves. The new technique used here is the half bend vibrato in the second line at draw hole 3.

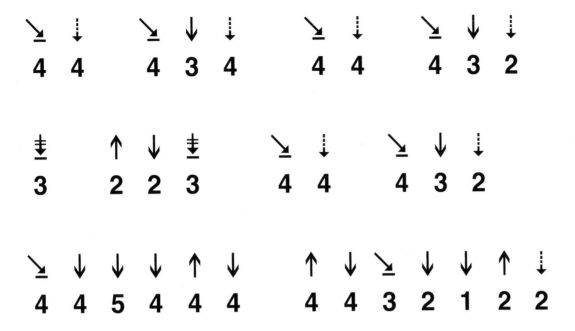

Here's a second solo to play over the blues shuffle. This one's a little busier than the previous example and contains some interesting bends and piano slides. Once you've got both blues solos down, put it all together into one continuous solo.

2nd Position – A Harmonica

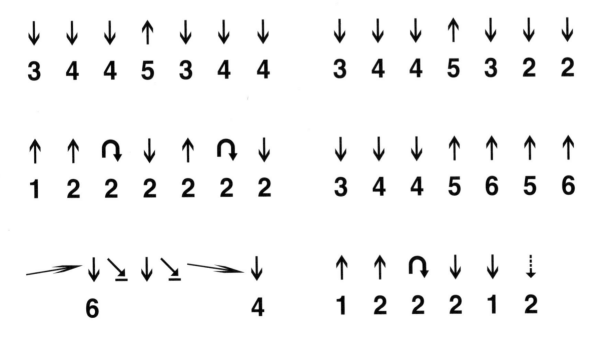

Canned Heat

At this point we'll start examining the styles of some world-class harmonica greats and legends. This section is in the style of Canned Heat's harmonica player Alan Wilson. We'll be using an A harmonica in 2nd position. The background rhythm track basically stays in an E blues feel throughout. The first solo below contains some good examples of bends and half step vibrato bends.

2nd Position – A Harmonica

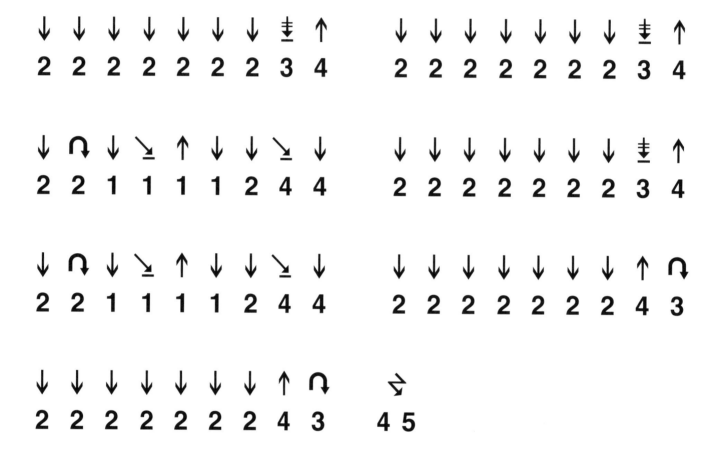

Here's a second solo that can be played over that same blues vamp. This one utilizes some classic trills followed by piano slides. There are also some more half step vibrato bends on long, sustained notes, giving you an opportunity to vary the speed and intensity of the vibrato.

2nd Position – A Harmonica

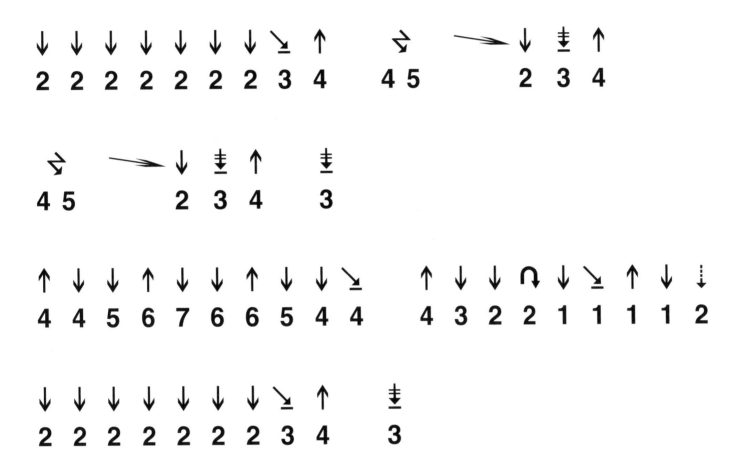

You can play these two solos back to back to create one long solo. Since the chord structure is the same repeated figure throughout, you can also separate the riffs and phrases and construct your own solo. At this point you should be comfortable with all of these techniques, and with playing in 2nd position. Start trying to come up with your own ideas and original solos.

Huey Lewis

Let's play some standard Huey Lewis–style rock and roll. The song is in the key of A, so we'll be using a D harp for the first time. The solo below contains some octaves in the second line, represented by the stacked numbers.

2nd Position – D Harmonica

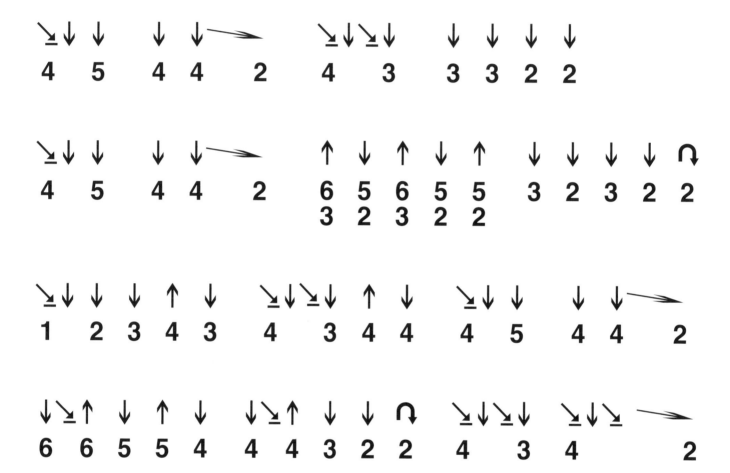

This second solo example uses most of the techniques you've learned up till now. The chords with half step bends are used here to create the same train sound that was used in the Beatles example earlier. There are also quite a few piano slides and worbles to make this a fun, interesting solo. Once you've got this second example down, play it consecutively with the previous one to create one long solo.

2nd Position – D Harmonica

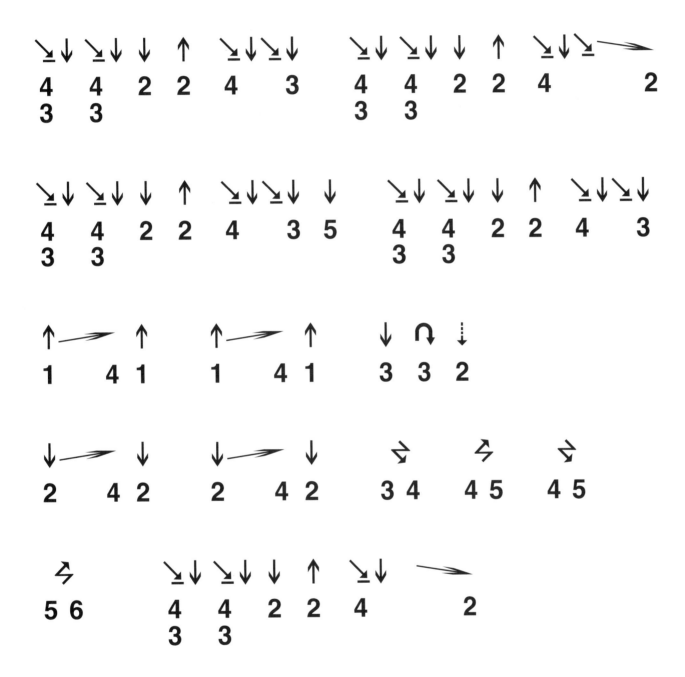

Bonnie Raitt

Now let's take a look at some examples that switch harmonicas to accommodate the chord changes. These solos are in the style of Norton Buffalo, Bonnie Raitt's harmonica player back in the '70s. The song is in C minor and the chords change in a descending progression Cm-B♭-A♭-G. We're going to use a technique called "chasing the changes" and switch to a different harmonica for each chord. All of the harmonicas will be played in 2nd position and are indicated above each line of the example. You can perform this on the four harmonicas by stacking two harmonicas in each hand.

2nd Position – F Harmonica

2nd Position – E♭ Harmonica

4 5   4 4 2

2nd Position – D♭ Harmonica

1 2 3 4 3   1 2 3 4

2nd Position – C Harmonica

4 3 4 4   4 3 4

1 2 3 4 3   4 3 4 4

While a chord progression like this lends itself very well to using multiple harps, you can also play a perfectly acceptable solo using only one. Here's another example played on just the F harp.

2nd Position – F Harmonica

4   5 4 6 5   4   2   2 1

↗ ↓ ↓ ↑ ↓ ↑ ↓   ↗ ↓ ↑ ↓ ↓ ↓ ↓
  5 5 5 4 5 4   5 5 4 5 4 5

↑ ↓ ↓ ↑ ↓ ↘⃗   ↑ ↓ ↓
6 5 4 6 5 4 5   6 5 4

↘↓↘↓ ↘↓↘↓ ⟶   ↓ ↑ ↓ ↘↓↘↓
4 3 4 3   1 1 2 2 3 2

Here's another solo using all four harps chasing the changes. Once you've got this one down, string it together with the first example and play it as one long solo.

2nd Position – F Harmonica

↑ ↓ ↓ ↓ ↓   ↓ ⤴ ↓ ↓
6 5 4 5 4   2 2 1 2

2nd Position – E♭ Harmonica

↑ ↑ ↓ ↑ ↓ ↓ ↓ ↓ ↓ ↓ ↑ ↓
6 5 4 5 4 3 4 3 2 2 1 2

2nd Position – D♭ Harmonica

↓ ↑ ↑ ↓ ↓ ↑ ↑   ↓ ↓ ↑ ↑ ↓
1 2 3 3 4 5 6   7 6 6 5 4

2nd Position – C Harmonica

↘↓ ↓ ↓ ↓ ↑ ↓   ↘↓ ↓ ↓ ↓   ⟶ ↓
3 4 4 4 5 2 3   4 4 4   2

Bonnie Raitt *cont.*

Since the song is actually in C minor, we can also create another solo over the changes in 3rd position using a B♭ harmonica.

3rd Position – B♭ Harmonica

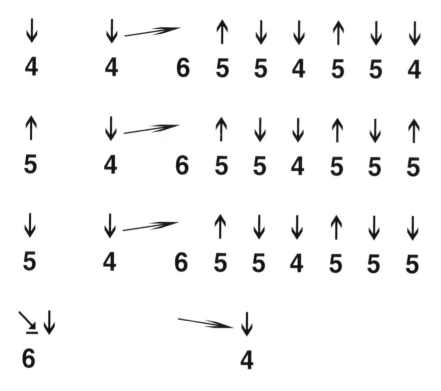

Stevie Wonder

Our final selection is in the style of Stevie Wonder, played in the key of A in first position. This example explores the upper register of the harp and introduces some blow-note bends. These bends are achieved by overblowing the note and dramatically increasing the airflow. The smaller *u*-shaped arrows in the these examples indicate slight grace note bends.

1st Position – A Harmonica

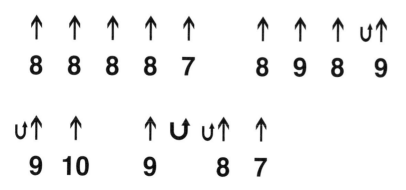

Here's a variation of the first solo that extends a little more into the lower register. After you've got this second one down, put it together with the first solo to create one continuous solo.

Ist Position – A Harmonica

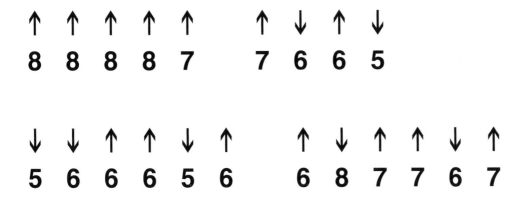

↑ ↑ ↑ ↑ ↑   ↑ ↓ ↑ ↓
8 8 8 8 7   7 6 6 5

↓ ↓ ↑ ↑ ↓ ↑   ↑ ↓ ↑ ↑ ↓ ↑
5 6 6 6 5 6   6 8 7 7 6 7

This third example contains elements of the first solo, but is played with a more syncopated, staccato feel. Play around with all three of these solos and create your own variations.

Ist Position – A Harmonica

↑ ↑ ↑ ↑   ↑ ↑ ↑ ↑ ↻↑ ↑ ↑
8 8 9 8   8 8 9 9 9 8 8 7

↻↑ ↑   ↑ ↻ ↻↑ ↑
9 10   9   8 7

Learning all of the techniques and songs in this book has hopefully kicked your harmonica playing up to the next level and given you a thorough background to the world of rock harmonica. We've explored numerous techniques and shown you how to play in different positions and in different registers. You can apply all of the riffs, tricks, and information to help guide you in creating your own style.

Ten Hole Harmonica Key Chart

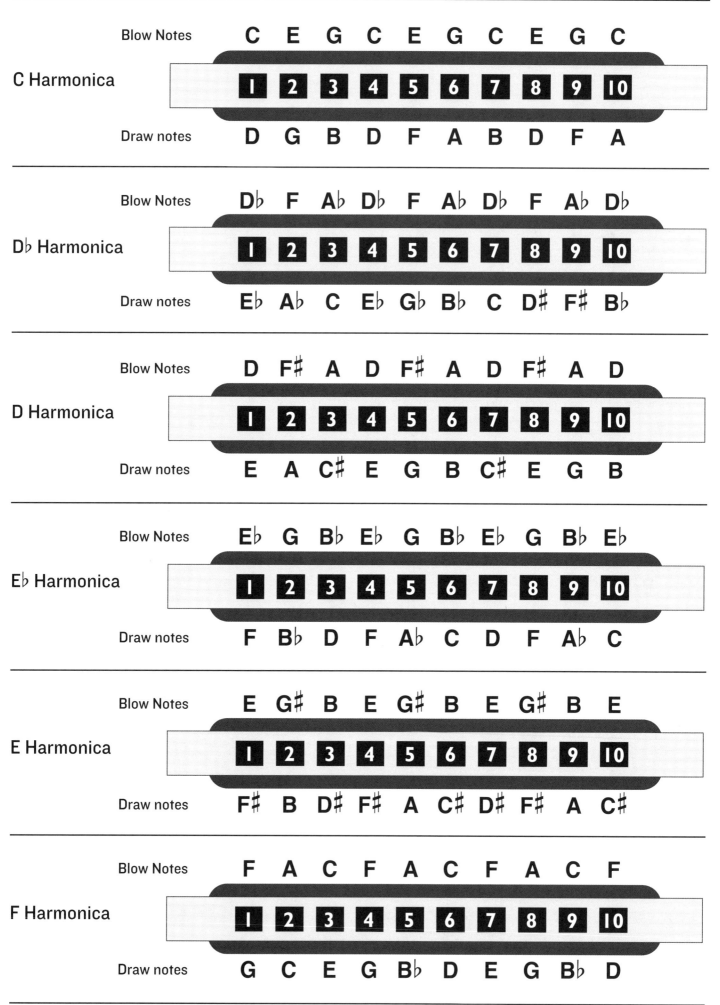

C Harmonica

Blow Notes: C E G C E G C E G C
1 2 3 4 5 6 7 8 9 10
Draw notes: D G B D F A B D F A

Db Harmonica

Blow Notes: Db F Ab Db F Ab Db F Ab Db
1 2 3 4 5 6 7 8 9 10
Draw notes: Eb Ab C Eb Gb Bb C D# F# Bb

D Harmonica

Blow Notes: D F# A D F# A D F# A D
1 2 3 4 5 6 7 8 9 10
Draw notes: E A C# E G B C# E G B

Eb Harmonica

Blow Notes: Eb G Bb Eb G Bb Eb G Bb Eb
1 2 3 4 5 6 7 8 9 10
Draw notes: F Bb D F Ab C D F Ab C

E Harmonica

Blow Notes: E G# B E G# B E G# B E
1 2 3 4 5 6 7 8 9 10
Draw notes: F# B D# F# A C# D# F# A C#

F Harmonica

Blow Notes: F A C F A C F A C F
1 2 3 4 5 6 7 8 9 10
Draw notes: G C E G Bb D E G Bb D

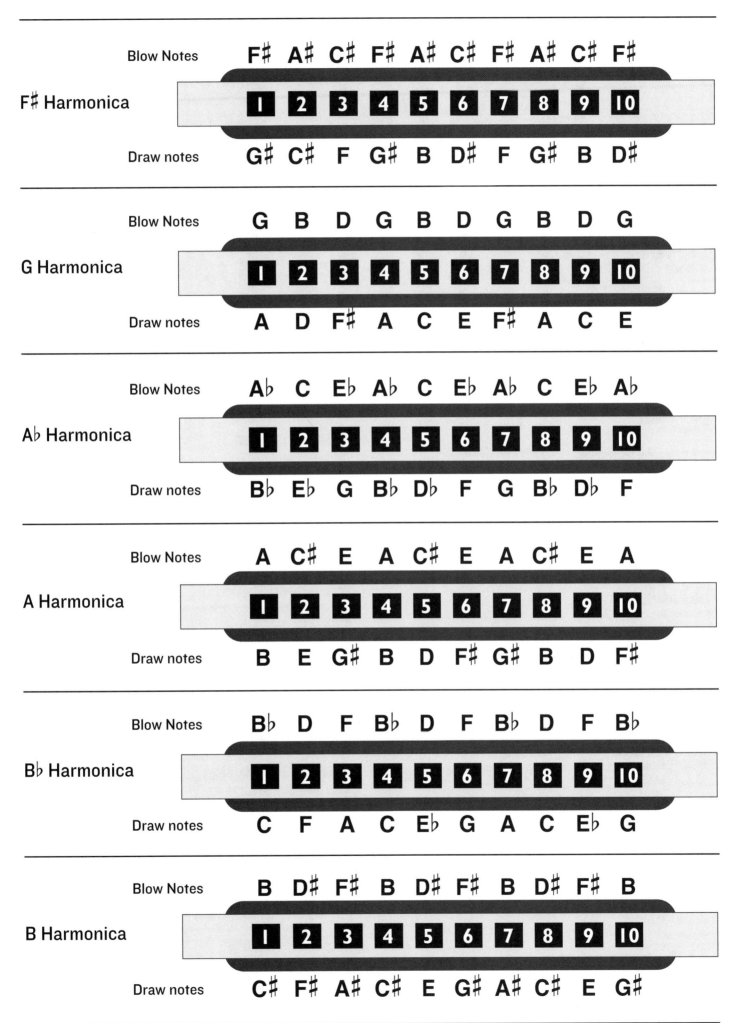

Great DVD selections from CHERRY LANE

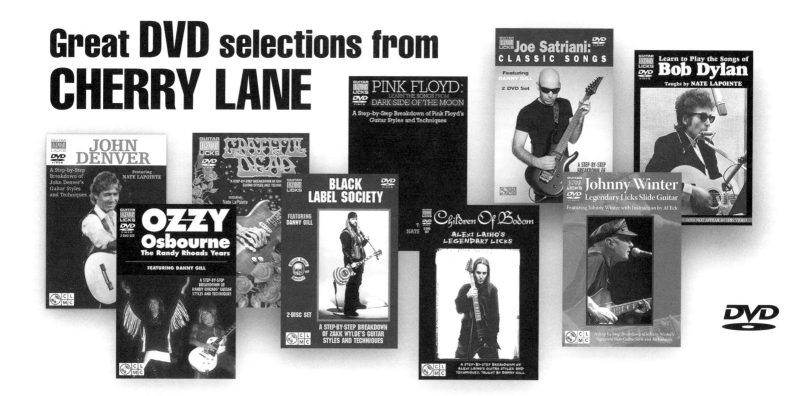

Steven Adler's Getting Started with Rock Drumming
taught by the Legendary Former Guns N' Roses Drummer!
02501387 DVD $19.99

Altered Tunings and Techniques for Modern Metal Guitar
taught by Rick Plunkett
02501457 DVD $16.99

Beginning Blues Guitar
RHYTHM AND SOLOS
taught by Al Ek
02501325 DVD $19.99

Black Label Society
featuring Danny Gill
Guitar Legendary Licks
02500983 2-DVD Set $19.99

Blues by the Bar
MORE AUTHENTIC LICKS BY THE BLUES MASTERS
taught by Danny Gill
02501477 DVD $16.99

Blues Masters by the Bar
taught by Dave Celentano
02501146 DVD $24.99

Children of Bodom
ALEXI LAIHO'S LEGENDARY LICKS
taught by Danny Gill
02501398 DVD $16.99

John Denver
featuring Nate LaPointe
Guitar Legendary Licks
02500917 DVD $16.99

Learn to Play the Songs of Bob Dylan
taught by Nate LaPointe
Guitar Legendary Licks
02500918 DVD $16.99

Funky Rhythm Guitar
taught by Buzz Feiten
02501393 DVD $24.99

Grateful Dead – Classic Songs
featuring Nate LaPointe
Guitar Legendary Licks
02500968 DVD $24.95

Grateful Dead
featuring Nate LaPointe
Guitar Legendary Licks
02500551 DVD $24.95

The Latin Funk Connection
02501417 DVD $16.99

Metallica – 1983-1988
featuring Doug Boduch
Bass Legendary Licks
02500481 DVD $16.99

Metallica – 1988-1997
featuring Doug Boduch
Bass Legendary Licks
02500484 DVD $16.99

Metallica – 1983-1988
featuring Nathan Kilen
Drum Legendary Licks
02500482 DVD $16.99

Metallica – 1988-1997
featuring Nathan Kilen
Drum Legendary Licks
02500485 DVD $16.99

Metallica – 1983-1988
featuring Doug Boduch
Guitar Legendary Licks
02500479 DVD $16.99

Metallica – 1988-1997
featuring Doug Boduch
Guitar Legendary Licks
02500480 DVD $24.99

Mastering the Modes for the Rock Guitarist
taught by Dave Celentano
02501449 DVD $19.99

Home Recording Magazine's 100 Recording Tips and Tricks
STRATEGIES AND SOLUTIONS FOR YOUR HOME STUDIO
02500509 DVD $16.99

Ozzy Osbourne – The Randy Rhoads Years
featuring Danny Gill
Guitar Legendary Licks
02501301 2-DVD Set $29.99

Pink Floyd – Learn the Songs from Dark Side of the Moon
by Nate LaPointe
Guitar Legendary Licks
02500919 DVD $16.99

Rock Harmonica
taught by Al Ek
02501475 DVD $16.99

Poncho Sanchez
featuring the Poncho Sanchez Latin Jazz Band
02500729 DVD $24.95

Joe Satriani
featuring Danny Gill
Guitar Legendary Licks Series
02500767 2-DVD Set $29.95

Joe Satriani – Classic Songs
featuring Danny Gill
Guitar Legendary Licks
02500913 2-DVD Set $29.95

Johnny Winter
taught by Al Ek
Guitar Legendary Licks
02501307 2-DVD Set 29.99

Johnny Winter
SLIDE GUITAR
featuring Johnny Winter with instruction by Al Ek
Guitar Legendary Licks
02501042 DVD $29.95

Wolfmother
featuring Danny Gill
02501062 DVD $16.99

cherry lane music company